Some
to Start

Prayers by

Harry Undy

ISBN 0 85346 208 9

Prayers by Harry Undy

Published by Granary Press
the imprint of The United Reformed Church
86 Tavistock Place, London WC1H 9RT

Produced by Communications and Editorial, Graphics Office

Printed by Healeys Printers, Unit 10, The Sterling Complex, Farthing Road, Ipswich, Suffolk IP1 5AP

Contents

Timely Words 1

Morning 2

Evening 15

Christian Year 31

The Word & Words 41

Praise, Thanksgiving & Confession 51

Partial Conversations 61

Offering & Commitment 89

Foreword

I would like to thank the people who have brought this to print:
The good friends and collegues in the ecumenical life of Zimbabwe who pressed me for copies of prayers that were not even written down and made me work at re-usable prayers of general applicability;
Ben Ngidi who gave me the shock of hearing my own words being used in another voice when he was chairman of UCCSA Assembly;
Marion Morling who assured me that they still work in twenty-first century UK;
Edmund Banyard who offered advice on making the material ready for United Reformed Church publication.
To all these, heartfelt thanks.

Somewhere to Start

This collection of prayers offers somewhere to start in approaching God with the interests and concerns of everyday human life lived in faith. God does not need an invitation to think about us; God loves us and wills what is good for us whether or not we believe or care.

The selection has been made from prayers developed over some thirty years, starting in pre-independence Zimbabwe. Some of these prayers were originally designed for use with small groups of people who had worked intensely together and had become a community for a brief while.

It is hoped that all of them will give such a small community or an individual a good starting point from which they can develop a dialogue with God, including comfort, challenge, correction and fun. If such a dialogue does develop, there is no off switch; God is likely to pick up the threads again at any time in what you read, in casual conversations, in sudden realisations of what is seen.

In several prayers there is an obvious response; this has not been indicated in the typesetting but has been left as an option for group use. Because of the difficulty sometimes met in trying to make inclusive language sound well, a convention of the translations of the Old Testament into English has been adopted in several places; "LORD" is used to represent the name of God.

Where is the midwife, Jesus?

She is not in the gospel nativity story;
I don't remember seeing her in any great painting
(though she might have been
in the murky background of one or two);
she does not appear in the nativity play.
But she must have been there when you were born.

Why has she been air-brushed out?
Who decided that she was not quite decent or proper?
Who cleaned up the birth to make it nicely religious?

If the crying and the effort and the mess
of your birth do not have a part in faith,
I will have to watch myself;
I won't be able to share with you
my crying and my effort and my messes.
I will have to pretend you do not know me as I am.
I will censor and filter,
I will approach you with a mask on
and hide from myself the truth you show me.

But you are Truth.
You love *me*.
If you ever showed me myself, as you know me,
I would be shattered
(except you always show me in love).

So bring back the midwife
and help me to pray out of the fullness of my life
so that you are within every part of me.

Timely words

morning

and
evening

and
the Christian year

The night has ended and the day begun.
Thank you, LORD.
After dark we are glad in the light of the sun.
Thank you LORD.
New work now is waiting to be done.
Thank you LORD.

For all your gifts throughout our life,
Thank you LORD.
For peace of heart in a world of strife,
Thank you LORD.
For truth to cut through lies like a knife,
Thank you LORD.

With the past forgiven we start anew.
Thank you LORD.
You have promised us strength if we trust in you.
Thank you LORD.
Please help us today, in all we do, to
Thank you LORD.

Morning thanks

LORD, I do not know
what today will bring, nor how I will meet the events.

I do know that in your service
I am free,
not a slave to evil,
not a slave to myself,
but truly free.

Guard this freedom for me today, LORD.

Prepare me to face attacks
from the enemy
whether they are strongest
from outside myself or
from my own selfishness.
Prepare me to trust in your strength.

Whatever today brings to my life,
keep me free for your service
in joy.

Morning trust

Jesus said, "Love God
and love your neighbour."
John said: "My children, love one another
for love is of God."

Lord Jesus Christ,
we know that love is the way you act towards us,
love is your own nature.

We want to obey your commands,
and we know that the first command is to love you,
and the second is to love our neighbour.
How can we do this, Lord?
How can our lives show your nature to others?

It is easy to love people we like;
easy to love people who help us;
easy to love people who respond to our love.
But some of the people we know are not like that.
It would be difficult to love all people.
And yet, Lord,
you loved the lepers,
you loved the Pharisees and the High priest,
you loved the Romans,
you loved nationalists and collaborators,
you loved extremists on all sides of all questions,
you loved old and young, rich and poor.
You even love each one of us, all the time,
even when we find it hard to love ourselves

And so Lord, please live in us today so that our love for others may not be just our own proud and feeble effort, but may be Jesus Christ living and loving in us.

A challenge of love

For the gift of the night and the gift of the day,
thank you LORD.
For the gift of speech and good things to say,
thank you LORD.
For a time of peace when we may pray,
thank you LORD.

For food and clothes and a roof and a bed,
thank you LORD.
For wood and brick and cloth and thread,
thank you LORD.
For knowledge and skill and labour shared,
thank you LORD.

For books to read, good things to see,
thank you LORD.
For pleasant air, for being free,
thank you LORD.
For all the care you give to me,
thank you LORD.

Please, LORD, take our thanks,
and as we use these good gifts of yours,
let our use and our thoughtfulness show our deep gratitude.

Morning thanks

Lord Jesus Christ, there is nothing very much that I can offer.

Even when I do my best, it is no more than I ought to do anyway, so I cannot expect or claim any credit for trying.

In any case, all my abilities and skills are your gifts to me, so that I can use them for a while in whatever way is pleasing to you. I have not made my own body or my own mind - I am part of your work of Creation.

What I have done too often is forget that I am yours, and I have used these powers in ways that I am ashamed of when I remember how you, Lord Jesus, used just the same sort of body as you have given me.

Please forgive me for being proud in a way that separates me from you.

Help me to remember that it is the humble who are blessed, and that I can be humble if I remember who I am and who you are.

On this new day, please Lord help me to use what you have lent me in a way that will show other people that I am yours. And help me to remember that I have prayed this prayer, so that I do not simply forget all that I want to do in your name.

By accepting me, Lord, your grace is enough to make me acceptable as an offering to you.

Morning confession

We rise in the morning,
the sun shines, and life is good;
Praise the Creator;
God gives us the good things of life.

All around are friends to help us, things to see,
new things to learn.
Praise the Creator;
God gives us the good things of life.

Our bodies have strength and health,
our minds have the power of thought.
Praise the Creator;
God gives us the good things of life.

God's earth provides our shelter, our clothing,
our books and all that we enjoy.
Praise the Creator;
God gives us the good things of life.

We know that there will be work and rest,
and games and talking and singing.
Praise the Creator;
God gives us the good things of life.

Help us today, loving God,
to live and give good lives to you.
Praise the Creator;
God gives us the good things of life.

Morning praise

Ruler of time and space, we do not know what today is bringing us, and we do not know what we shall be like at the end of the day.

If there is to be unexpected happiness, help us to share it with others, so that their lives too may be happier. Happiness is your gift, and Jesus brought it to so many people that we can know he is present with us also in our happiness.

If there is sadness, help us by sharing it with us, carrying our load again as you have done so often. Help us to serve you by doing this service to those around us who are sad, offering them your strength through our love.

If there is work to be done, help us to do it to the best of our ability, so that we do not bring trouble and disappointment to others, and so that we do not store up trouble for ourselves.

If there is to be a chance to do something to help our neighbour, make us see that chance, and help us to do whatever Jesus would do, so that we do not have to try to hide from you, because we cannot hide from you however hard we try - it's easier to do the right thing to begin with.

At the end of the day, may we look back over what has happened to us, and the ways we have happened to others, and not be ashamed to thank you and praise you in prayer.

Morning hope

Thanks be to you, Lord Christ,
for making yourself known to us.
God in our form,
Almighty Saviour in our limits.

You were in the act of creation,
and through you all is made new.
and all is brought to completion.

We thank you for all creation
and for the love which binds your work together.
We thank you for the Word
given in life and witness for our strength and faith.
We thank you for the church,
in all ages and in all lands your body,
victorious over death.
We thank you
that your majesty is far beyond our measure
or our comprehension.

And we thank you, each one,
aware of what we have received in our lives
of your loving generosity.

Thanks be to you, Lord Christ.

Morning thanks

Each new day is your gift, loving living God;
We praise you,
all your gifts are good.

Darkness for sleep and light for work are your gifts;
We praise you,
all your gifts are good.

Brain and eye and hand are your gifts;
We praise you,
all your gifts are good.

Food and drink and all materials for use are your gifts;
We praise you,
all your gifts are good.

The help other people give us is your gift;
We praise you,
all your gifts are good.

The opportunities to do good today are your gifts;
We praise you,
all your gifts are good.

Life and faith and understanding and hope are your gifts;
We praise you,
all your gifts are good.

Friendship and joy and sorrow are your gifts;
We praise you,
all your gifts are good.

May our lives today be praise for you, so that the world may be happier for our presence.

Morning praise

Loving, generous God
prodigal with your love
you give us more than we can measure;
you offer us more than we can receive;
you bestow good gifts beyond our comprehension.

From you we have our lives,
our love and our hope,
our faith and our questions,
our memories and our expectations
- you enable us to be your people,
you bless us by calling us your children.

We thank you for your gifts:
for your calling and your presence;
for this world and your eternity;
for all that is good.

Again in this new day
we marvel that you sustain us in your loving-kindness
and we offer ourselves to you.

Morning praise

Loving God, our Creator, Judge and Saviour
we offer to you this time of morning worship.

We worship you because you help us to know you, and the better we know you,
in your love, your generosity, your strength,
the more we want to acknowledge that we are your people.

We are yours because you create us.
We live because of you,
we have this planet and our family and friends because of you.

We are yours because you judge us.
You know every part of our lives better than we know ourselves,
and we live in the light of your perfection.

We are yours because you save us.
You know we cannot save ourselves
and so you offer all that we need just because you love us.

And yet, God, though we know you and your love,
we have not really obeyed you.
We confess that we have disappointed you
and have fallen away from the right course.
We have treated other people as of less value than ourselves,
we have used them in our selfishness
and we have not accepted your strength
to walk in the way of love.

As you have promised forgiveness
to those who turn to you away from sin,
help us to trust you, to receive your salvation
and to become new again in your service

For morning worship

God of life and love,
we thank you for the morning,
for the sun and the showers, for the warmth and the wind,
for the new growth and the flowers,
for the hopes of spring with all the beauty and the new life.
We are glad
because you, God, have made a world
which provides so many good things
and you create us able to know its glory.

Most of all, on this day,
we thank you for the life of Jesus,
lived as fully human,
given on the cross in love
and given again by your power for our sakes.

Christ is risen
and you call us to live in him,
in the glory of eternal life.

We are sorry for the way
we have helped to spoil your world's glory.
For greed and selfishness;
for taking too much and caring too little
when others do not have any;
for saying "It's nothing to do with me"
when we know we are to love our neighbour as ourselves.

Keep your promise, judging, loving God;
forgive us if we are truly sorry
and want to live in love,
and help us to know
that we can call on your strength for life abundant.

Sunday morning thanks

How can we know
that you are here, risen Lord?

This is a time for talking to you, but it must not be a one-way monologue, with you just listening. The easiest sin to commit is to call this a time of prayer and then ignore you.

Let us hear you in the sounds of the world's activities around us; you will speak to us through other people, and through the busy-ness of serving of all kinds.
Please teach us to serve others, Lord, even in ways like the washing of your disciples' dirty feet.

Let us know your readiness to forgive our sins in our own awakening today, with another chance to tell you we are sorry for our disobedience to your command to love God and to love our neighbour.
As we feel the strength in our bodies, so also let us feel your strength to help us fight temptation.

In the new ideas and knowledge as we learn today, Lord, let us realise that you are ready to show yourself to us in truth, and help us to judge all things by the standard of your truth.

All through today, Lord, please help us to be not too proud to hear you speak to us in whatever way you choose, and do not let our pride refuse to know you when you do not come in ways we demand.

Approach

Lord Jesus,
accept what I have done today,
accept what I have been today,
accept me as I have become
through today's living.

Forgive the wrong in my life today,
and give me peace through faith
in your forgiveness;
not taking it lightly,
because forgiveness for me
cost your life,
but taking your promise truly
with no more nursing of my sins.

Please, Lord,
grant me rest
so that I may be strong
to help repair tomorrow
the damage I have done today,
by serving you in love.

to you be all praise and glory.

Evening commitment

Thank you, God.

Thank you for giving me the morning
and for every day that's new
and for carrying my heaviest burdens.

Thank you for all my friends,
for my brothers and sisters,
for my parents,
for all great people
and even for my enemies.

Thank you for the company of people around me,
for living and learning,
for pleasure and music
and light and happiness.

Thank you for joy and for sorrows,
and for the kindness I receive in my sorrow
and for your guidance all the time.

Thank you, God, for speaking to me
in so many different ways;
help me to listen
and to hear.

Please give me good and safe rest this night
and all such things as you know I need.

In the name of Jesus Christ.

Evening thanks

Help us now to remember, Lord,
what you told us about yourself.

You said;
"I am the Light":
give us your light
so that we might walk and sleep in safety.

You said;
"I am the Bread of Life for all humankind."
feed us
so that we might have strength to serve you.

You said;
"I am the Way and the Door."
help us to walk in your way all our lives
so that we may enter at the end as you want us to.

You said;
"I am the Good Shepherd, who lays down his life."
we are your sheep, you laid down your life for us,
keep us in peace this night.

You said;
"I am the Life."
please, Lord, give us that life
so that we might live a good life and a full life in this your world.

Forgive us for the times when we have refused your love today, Lord,
and by the love of your forgiveness
strengthen us to obey you tomorrow.

Evening petition

and we come to our Prayer of Praise

Let us praise God, our Maker and Lord.

God gives us food and water;
        Praise him with joy;
he gives us all that is good in life.

God gives us the sun to shine and the wind to blow,
heat and coolness;
        Praise him with joy;
he gives us all that is good in life.

God gives us work to do and strength to do it;
        Praise him with joy;
he gives us all that is good in life.

God gives us knowledge, and our lives are blessed with truth;
        Praise him with joy;
he gives us all that is good in life.

God gives us parents and family and friends;
        Praise him with joy;
he gives us all that is good in life.

God gives us life, and his will is that we should be happy;
        Praise him with joy;
he gives us all that is good in life.

God gave us this day, with all that has enriched our lives;
        Praise him with joy;
he gives us all that is good in life.

+ for this we give you thanks & praise Amen

God gives us this night, for rest and renewal;
        Praise him with joy;
he gives us all that is good in life.

Evening praise

O God,
LORD of day and night,
as you kept us safe through the day
so now keep us safe through the night.

You have been with us through today,
you have offered us guidance and protection;
be present and protect us through the silent hours,
and guide us till the morning light;
so that we,
who have been tired by the changes
and the activities of the day
may find rest
in the quiet certainty
and unchangeableness of your love.

And then, O God,
awake us again in the morning,
refreshed by our rest,
quickly aware of your calling,
and strong to serve you.

Through Christ our Saviour.

For safe keeping

Almighty God,
it is difficult to remember your greatness
- all-knowing, all-powerful, always and everywhere -
and at the same time to think that you
know about
and care about
and deal with
ordinary people
living ordinary and not especially good or holy lives.

Sometimes it seems in the darkness of the night
that we must have been left alone
to get on with things as best we may,
and if we make a mess of living,
then the darkness of the night will spread into our spirits.

Then, God, we need to be reminded that you are
not only the Almighty;
you are also Father and Mother
and you banish loneliness
for your children;
you are also Brother Christ
and God's love was strong enough
in your despair, deeper than we can ever know;
you are also Holy Spirit
and our lives and our world
are the places of your loving work.

Keep these thoughts in our minds
and your love in our hearts,
so that your grace and love and fellowship
will give us the light of faith
in the dark of the night and the dark of our fears.

Evening approach

Generous God
take our gifts
and make us fruitful sons and daughters.

You have given us love
and you have taught us to love.
By your grace,
strengthen our love for our neighbours,
make us eager to serve them
and to bring them into your Kingdom.

And now, loving and generous God,
take us into your care while we sleep,
grant us peaceful rest and good wakening,
so that we may rise in new enthusiasm
to serve you tomorrow.

Evening trust

O God, our Father and Friend,
we thank you for all the happiness of the day now ending.
We thank you for all who have been kind to us today,
who have helped us with their words, their sympathy or their example.

We thank you for work honestly done and games played well;
for friendship and fun; and for all good things.

Before we go to rest tonight,
we give ourselves into your loving care through Jesus Christ,
your Son and our Lord.

According to his promises,
forgive those things we have done wrong today,
by speaking or by silence, by act or stillness,
which we now confess and repent.

Make us clean from selfishness of all kinds,
and make us strong for the right.

Take us, and all whom we love,
into your care for the night.

Through Jesus Christ our Lord.

Evening thanks

To you, LORD God, we now commend ourselves,
and all whom we love.

Keep us in your care tonight,
and help us to know our unity in your love,
however far apart we may be.

Have pity on all sufferers,
whether their pain be in body or mind or spirit.
Give sympathy and skill to those
who care for them,
so that they may bring your comfort.

Teach us to bear each other's burdens,
so that we may be conductors
of the power of your love
to lighten the cares of others.

May truth, honour and kindness
grow among us.

May your blessing rest on our work,
making it acceptable to you.

May your name be honoured among us
and your peace guard our hearts
to strengthen all who call on you
now, through the night, and in the morning.

Through Jesus Christ our Saviour.

Evening petition

The Lord Jesus takes care of us,
when we're sleeping and when we're waking.

The Lord Jesus takes care of us,
when we're working and when we're learning,
when we're resting and when we're rushing.

Lord, wherever I go
    may your power protect me;
wherever they are,
    watch over my family;
wherever they are,
    watch over my friends and loved ones.

Tonight, Lord Jesus,
    may your love touch your people in distress:
where people are ill,
    heal their sickness;
where people are in trouble,
    help them according to their needs;
in the presence of your spirit,
    give us refuge and strength.

And in the days to come continue this work of love
for me, and in me, and though me for others.

Evening commitment

When we think of the day we have enjoyed,
we know how good God is to us.

We thank you, God.
Your goodness is not just for the few, but for all creation.

We pray for all who are ill
including any known to us:
especially for those who have suffered long;
and for those who society shuts out because of a disability.
Hear us now, O God;
and bless them, we pray.

We pray for those who are worried and afraid
including any known to us:
those who suffer ill health because of fears,
and those who care for them.
Hear us now, O God;
and bless them, we pray.

We pray for those who suffer because of sin
including any known to us:
their own sin or the sins of others,
and especially those who do not know you will forgive.
Hear us now, O God;
and bless them, we pray.

Grant to our own family and friends
and to all your people,
good rest in your care;
in Jesus' name.

Evening thanks and intercession

It has been a good day,
thank you, LORD God.

There have been so many things to enjoy,
I can't even remember them all;
I can't list them now to thank you by number.

But you were there each time, God.
You want me to be truly happy and satisfied,
so it is your will that good things happen
and you have known all about my today

When others have helped me,
giving me advice and sympathy,
helping me to do the difficult things,
helping me to avoid what is wrong;
you have known and rejoiced with me in my relief.

You have even helped me to help others,
putting aside my selfishness for a while,
loving my neighbour as I love myself.

It feels good to do good.
But the feeling inside me is not what really matters.
The important thing is that for a while,
some time, today,
I have done what you want me to do,
I have grown a bit more in love,
I have learned a bit more about life,
I have been who you want me to be.

It has been a good day today,
thank you, LORD God.

Evening thanks

God of all power and wisdom,
maker of earth and all on it and in it;
maker of the planets and the sun and the stars
and the deep voids of space;
we thank you for our lives and for all
you have given us.

God of love and peace,
Controller of nations and peoples and rulers;
Lord and Governor of history
and all that is to come;
we ask you to show us your way
so that we may serve you.

All praise and worship and service is yours, O God;
for the blessings we have received in the day now ending,
all thanks are yours.

So teach us to serve only you,
and then in all parts of our lives
we shall know peace and security and love;
and the rest we enjoy this night
will prepare us to serve you tomorrow.

We pray in Jesus' name.

Evening commitment

You have filled today with good things
for me, O Lord Jesus Christ.
Please forgive me
for not thanking you while I enjoyed them,
for preferring things which are worse,
for abusing some of your gifts.

You have provided all my senses,
and you have given something good for each one.

I have enjoyed things that are good to see,
things that are good to taste;
pleasant sounds have come to my ears;
I have touched good things
and there have been pleasing scents.

This body that you have planned and that you have given,
the human body that was good enough even for Jesus,
is a wonderful gift.
Please help me to use it well
to respect it and honour it as yours,
to respect and honour other people too,
and to rejoice in your generous practical love.

In tonight's rest, Lord,
please give me renewed strength
so that my body may be ready to serve you
and to find enjoyment in life tomorrow.
In serving others I serve you.
May my mind and my spirit be refreshed,
so that in the new day
I may be more aware of you in the splendour of your good gifts
and your will that life should be good.

Response to gifts

LORD God of love,
we bring you our praise and our requests.

We praise you
because your love has given us so much this day and every day;
food and shelter,
family and friends,
light and learning.

We know that your way is the way of peace and love,
where each person is my neighbour.

We ask you to give strength
to all who know you,
so that they may teach the world.
Break down hatred between people,
between nations and races and tribes,
between classes and societies and faiths.

Teach us true love and respect for each other in this community,
so that comforted by both our obedience to your love
and by your promise of forgiveness
to all who are truly sorry for their sins,
we may rest peacefully in the night.

In the name of Jesus our Saviour we ask it.

Praise and intercession

O Lord of the dance, yours is a dance of life, not of death.
Our lives should be a dance to the same tune,
the song of expectation and victory.
Christ is risen:
He is risen indeed.

Many are afraid, many will not sleep well tonight,
because fear is the enemy of peace and the end of hope.
This day we can know happiness,
tonight we can renew our strength for life in your service,
dancing with you.
Christ is risen:
He is risen indeed.

Some tell us there is no hope, no grounds for expectation;
they say there is nothing your Church can do;
the evil in humankind is too strong;
people's only wish is to destroy.
Christ is risen:
He is risen indeed.

But we meet here in your name, we find the steps you set for us;
we know that your strength exalts you above all evil
and suffering and death
and you lift your dancing partners with you.
Christ is risen:
He is risen indeed.

After they laid you in the tomb they sorrowed;
they did not know the infinity of your power.
We have no sorrow like that; we can live in hope and trust.
Your day of resurrection is our day of worship;
worship of the risen Lord, the Victor, the Dance-leader,
Christ is risen:
He is risen indeed.

Intercession

God of promise and delivery,
God of the busy family and the lonely individual,
God of feast and of famine,
all life is your gift and your concern
and in all life your will is for our good.

For those who can see angels
the heavenly choir brings your message;
for those who can hear their neighbours
the shepherds and the wise men, the mother and the inn keeper
speak for you;
for those who understand the silence of their own hearts
you come by night and by day
to comfort and to call your people.

In faith we bring our concerns to you,
that girls and boys, men and women may be set free
to sing your glory until the earth echoes with praise.

God who seeks need and gives in love,
we pray for those who are homeless,
feeling shut out and dismissed
from the comfortable society which gloats over its wealth.
For their sake bring reconciliation,
and break through the blindness of the self-satisfied
to open doors.

We pray for those who spend Christmas in fear,
not of angels singing glory
but of beatings and abuse,
of bombs and bullets and fire,
of the sack and poverty.
For their sake bring peace
with honesty and repentance
opening the way for hope and justice.

We pray for those who have no faith in you,
for whom this time is full of greed and frustration.
For their sake let songs of faith and praise be raised.
We pray for those who mourn and grieve
in a time of celebration,
seeing only the empty place and hearing only the silence.
For their sake may shyness be overcome
so that the comfort of your love comes in
through the open hearts of your people.

And now we pray for ourselves,
that we may be open to the love of our families and friends
and to the needs of our neighbours - because you love us.

Christmas

Now we make confession of our sins.

O God of mercy, as the year draws to its close,
we confess the weakness, failure and disobedience
of so many of its days;
our broken vows and frequent refusal of your guidance;
our slackness and misuse of time and opportunity;
our forgetfulness of our duty of love to you and to our neighbour;
our selfishness and sloth; our unkindness and indifference;
our blindness to your purpose in life;
our self-indulgence and our pleasure at the expense of others;
our feeble witness to all that you have given us;
our times of untruth;
our cowardice, our evasiveness and our hypocrisy;
our slowness to recognise the power of Christ in events;
our lack of faith in you.

For these sins, have mercy O God.
Forgive us, not because of our deserving
but because of your love and your promise.
Open our lives to this gift of yours,
and make us new.

Creator God, although the years change,
you are always God,
always our Saviour, always merciful,
always our sufficient Parent,
always mighty and always true.

You enter this New Year with us,
and we rejoice because we can still
trust in your help.
You are making this year
as you have made all that exists.

We thank you for the days
and months and years past,
with all the different flavourings
that make life good,
and we ask you to guide us,
teach us and strengthen us
in this year you - we - have now started.

Forgive our sins, dear God,
and make us new too,
ready and fit to serve you
with joy and hope.

Lord, on the day when we remember
your entry into Jerusalem,
we want to enter
into a community of worship
with each other and with you.

There is the shouting of the world,
the pressures to do what is expected,
to pick up today's fashion
and throw it down again tomorrow.
We hear it now as you heard it then.
We don't want to forget the world, Lord,
we belong to your world;
you made it, you love all your people,
and you understand.

With all the odd bits and pieces on our minds,
all the anxieties and ambitions,
receive these prayers.

Let us look over the things that come to mind,
the good and the sad, and ask God to deal with them.

(silence)

Lord, you went on into the city, ready to love and forgive;
please forgive what needs to be forgiven now,
and help us to know that your forgiveness is real
when our repentance is real.
Strengthen what needs to be strengthened,
and teach us to exercise our faith in preparing your way again.
Lord, throughout this worship,
help us to offer you our true service.

Palm Sunday

The care of a chiropodist
is just about acceptable;
we make sure our feet have been washed first
before corns and bunions and hard skin
and ingrowing toe nails
are dealt with.
And it is the chiropodist's job.

But for your disciples
the washing of filthy smelly feet,
straight off the foul roads
and the stinking alleyways of the town
was the job of the slave.

Was this a test for them as well as a blessing?
Over the months
they had learned to call you Master
even when they thought you had some odd ideas.
A Master, a Rabbi, a Teacher - a Lord, even;
and you stripped off and took the bowl and the towel
like the lowest of the low,
not even a paid servant.

We cannot fit this into our ideas of a true leader,
so we will have to fit our ideas of a true leader
into your actions.
It is going to be embarrassing to us
as it was to them
so please help us to know you as you choose
to show yourself,
and to follow you with joy.

Maundy Thursday

Where would I have been, Lord?

I don't think I would have made it
right into the courtyard
to watch and be seen
and be challenged
It would not have been me who denied you;
I wouldn't have been anywhere near.

I suppose I might have made it
into the crowd on the hill;
that would have been anonymous enough,
there were lots of casual passers by
taking in the day's entertainment.

Each one of your disciples -
the apostles, the women and men -
who stayed by you
must have been a help, an assurance
that you had touched their lives.
Even the thief on the cross who recognised you
was a companion. He could not leave.
But then, even the Father seemed to leave you.

But you do not leave me.

I cannot understand your love.
But I can know it,
however much I fear I would desert you
and know I do not deserve you.
Make your presence real for me
in peace and joy.

Good Friday

Eternal Father God,
on this day of our Saviour's appearance
in new life,
setting out the truth of your love,
the love of your power,
the power of your Creation,
bring us again into the community
of your new life,
and teach us to pray.

We pray for those who deny life;
who exclude sisters and brothers
- your children -
for reasons of race, age, sex, education or wealth;
who limit their love by maintaining
their power and privilege
at the expense of the weak;
who choose ways of violence
and tear the life from people
and communities.
O Christ, may the light of your
resurrection life pour on them.

We pray for all to whom you have granted
privilege and duty of proclaiming your Gospel
(all your people, of high or low esteem);
that we may follow your Spirit
wherever you lead us,
being of comfort to the troubled,
being of challenge to the satisfied,
being living witness to your presence.

Easter

Christ is Risen!

How many people have proclaimed your life
since you were raised from death?
In how many situations of despair and gloom
of hope and joy,
has your new life been acclaimed?
Against persecution and propaganda,
against pressures to embrace greed and selfishness,
against all that is opposed to abundant life
Christ is risen! He is risen indeed!!

This old story is new again.
This turn-around of history is effective again.
This shock is disturbing again
and it is happening in my life
in my day and my world.

Life in the Life-giver
is greater than death;
there is no extinction of hope
for those who believe and accept.
Eternal Life does not await the end
but is the quality of your gift now.
I am made new;
the world is made new;
Christ is Risen.

Quicken the faith within me
so that my life proclaims what my lips speak:
Christ is Risen indeed!

Easter Day

Was it just the enthusiasm of the early days, Lord,
that produced all that noise and excitement
and running into the street and accosting passers-by
and having to defend themselves against
drunk -and-disorderly charges?
Or is that the way it ought to be
all the time, every time,
whatever the situation and the people?

There is that other story, in John's Gospel,
where you simply breathed on your disciples
and told them to receive that same Holy Spirit.
and it was so.

Perhaps you are working in your usual way,
knowing how we are all different
and meeting us and dealing with us in the way that is
best for us.

But you do not let us off the hook.
I am not allowed just to say
"I don't feel comfortable with that" and opt right out.
Without a full measure of your Spirit I cannot serve you
and I cannot believe and refuse to serve.
So, however it will be
renew your Spirit within me with power,
enable me for your service
so that I am yours in peace and joy
and obedience
to proclaim you in your world by my words and my living.

Pentecost

The Word & Words

Dear God, we use words now in our prayers
because words are our tools of shared communication.
Help our words to reflect our faith.

We pray for people who are made to fear words:
because all they ever hear is criticism and contempt;
because they are subjected to threats and abuse;
because all they know is hatred and despite.
May your Word comfort and restore them.

We pray for those who exploit word power,
with no love for truth:
those who promise, with no commitment;
those who praise, with no sincerity;
those who preach division and violence and deceit.
May your Word judge and correct them.

We pray for those who live by words,
who are tempted by their power:
for broadcasters and news reporters, with authority;
for authors and commentators, with persuasion;
for politicians and advertisers, with special pleading.
May your Word call them to truth and humility.

We pray for those who seek to serve your Word:
for Bible translators, interpreters, teachers;
for preachers, prayers and evangelists;
for those who seek to be faithful in reading and speaking
and living your Word.
May your Word dwell in them with the power they need.

Intercessions for word users

Thank you, speaking God;
thank you for your Word.

Thank you for your Word of Creation.
That all things you made are good,
and that all good things are your work.
Family love; enjoyment of true knowledge; wisdom;
happy friendships; food, health and play.
For the rest of the night and the enjoyment of the day
to you, LORD Creator, we give thanks.

Thank you for your Word in the Bible.
Your work of instruction and teaching that you patiently give
over many centuries and cultures,
so that your people may know you and know your will
and serve you and find joy and fulfilment in your service.
All this has been kept for us and brought to us;
men and women have studied and lived by this Word
and the wealth of their work is ours if we will accept it.
For guidance in your way, to you LORD Teacher we give thanks.

Thank you for your living Word, for Jesus Christ.
He was the power of Creation, he is the power of life;
he brings us liberty from the prison of sin.
Jesus can be so much more than just a name:
if we trust him, he will live with us in never-failing friendship;
he has taken away the pains our sin deserves;
he does this because he loves us
and still he loves us though we cause his suffering.
For the Word, the Way of Life,
we thank you Creator Saviour God.

Thanks for the word

Lord Jesus, you taught the people your truth
in parables and signs of power,
so that they might think and learn and understand.

Help us, day by day,
to see how you are teaching us
the same lessons about your love and goodness
to call us into service as disciples.

As we learn the rightness and order of number,
as we learn the unity of the lives of people
in all places and times,
as we enjoy the beauty and wealth of words,
as we learn more of the generosity
with which you created this universe,
show us also your truth and your majesty and your beauty
standing out against the chaos.

To those who humbly look for truth,
you reveal yourself, Lord.
O God our Creator and our Teacher,
we praise and thank you
and offer ourselves to learn and to serve.

For learning

Ah, but our difficulties are so great!

Yes, we have heard the Word.
It has been spoken to us,
and would have awoken in us a great response,
but our difficulties are so great.

Other people do not have
such difficulties.
It is easy for them to give
of their money and their time and their lives,
and we are very glad that we have had
so much from them.
It was, it is, easy for them
but ah, our difficulties are so great!

We are good receivers.
We open both hands for gifts.
From you, God, we have life and health and possessions
and help from friend and stranger.
But as for ourselves:
our difficulties are so great.

When we have bought what we need -
drinks and sweets and discs and cosmetics and petrol -
we might spare a few pence;
but it cannot be too much -
we let you have the change, God, because we never know when
an urgent demand might come.
The oddments of our time and money and lives are enough.

We would serve you, God, fully and enthusiastically,
but ah, our difficulties are so great!

Confession and Petition

If Christ is living now
(and I am sure he is)
surely he would keep his vow
and lead us into truth.

If Christ is working here
(and I am sure he is)
surely we would have less fear
of hate and evil lies.

If Christ is really real
(and I am sure he is)
the pride and envy that we feel
can still be overcome.

The present, living power
we find in Jesus Christ
can strengthen us in every hour
and give us victory.

Our enemy is known;
the living lie that tempts,
but even this is overthrown
by Jesus Christ alone.

It's Christ who gives us peace
(we can be sure it is)
so we can see his strength increase
in us when we obey.

Seeking Christ's truth

If a drum
is to give rhythm and life and meaning
to a song,
it must be warmed and brought to life.

My life is like a dead drum.
It does not sound and resound to your beat,
O LORD,
and it does not fit in
to the strong rhythm of life as you plan it.

Make me warm and alive, LORD;
warm in your service,
warm in heart and spirit
by sharing your joy.
Rouse me early in the day;
prepare me, ready for your feast of life

Help me to play my part
in that joyful insistent beat of life
that is your will.

You told us
that your kingdom is like a feast.
May my life
be part of the music of that feast
to your glory and praise.

Commitment to Life

When you came with your disciples
to the temple in Jerusalem,
they asked you admire the stones,
thinking of the great labour and long thought
given to erecting such a structure.
You were not much impressed, Lord.

We would probably invite you to admire our committees:
what a towering structure;
how many hours from how many people;
how many interconnecting channels;
and how much paper.
What do you think of this, Lord?

Help us to do today what is needful.
Help us to leave to you what is best left to you;
to know what needs to be said and what does not;
to know what can be left for one without everyone meddling;
to spare other people the ceaseless flow
of my thoughts, my ideas, my suggestions, my words.

Confirm our right decisions
and sterilise our mistakes,
so that we may bring glory to you, Jesus Christ our Lord.

Commitment

When you've got your telly and a full belly
and a car and a three piece suite
and a three piece suit and a second car
and a sound roof to your house
and a bar with fancy drinks to impress visitors
and your barns are full
and you have eaten and drunk and been merry:
what then?

You have filled your purse,
you have filled your house,
you have filled your body,
but what if your life is empty?

You can build up a nice warm glow inside,
because you know how good you have been;
you have given to good causes (even unpopular ones)
(even if you don't get a sticker to show for it).
The course you follow
is straight and righteous
and normal and safe and boring
and your life is still empty.

Your life
in the strife of this world
can be like a brass cymbal -
like all the top groups
all amplified together at a rave -
and it will still be empty
unless you have
love.

Challenge to Commit

Pressures are strongest
when they are subtle.
The small twist in the report,
the irrelevant almost-promise in the commercial,
the glaring headline which does not match the news,
the smear in the comment,
the damnation by association,
the licence of the cartoon
and the re-definition of words.

Usually reliable sources have their own axes to grind -
or perhaps they are grinding knives ready for someone's back.

"I am the Way, the Truth, the Life."

It makes the efforts of the Public Relations adviser
and the commentator and the copy writer
look a bit forced and small.

Let us reflect your light, God,
into the shadows cast by the opinion formers
and see what lurks there
for the sake of your truth and peace.

Seeking Truth

Praise, Thanksgiving & Confession

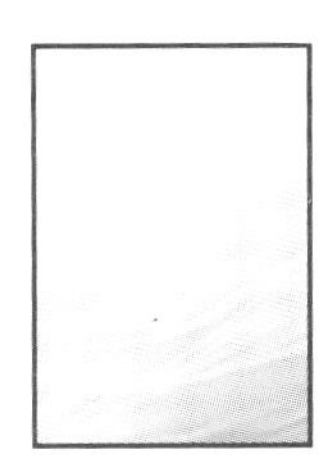

All praise belongs to you, O God, Creator.
Lord of history; past present and future;
Ruler over Kings and Government;
the only source of Truth and Wisdom.

May I praise you in my living,
may I praise you in my learning,
may I praise you in my loving,
may I praise you in my yearning.

As everything is yours, O God,
so may all creation praise you in joyful obedient love.

Praise

Loving, generous God,
you give us more than we can measure;
you offer us more than we will receive.

From you we have our lives,
our love and our hope,
our faith and our questions,
our memories and expectations
- you enable us to be people

We thank you for your gifts:
for your calling and your presence;
for this world and your eternity;
for all that is good.

Help us to hear you.

Help us to be open to all that you want to give us;
to accept all that is rich and good
so that we are set up to serve you
in the ways to which you call us,
knowing that you give before you call
but you do both give and call.

Thanks and Offering

My understanding is limited, O God,
so please help me to thank you.
I know that you have given me my life,
my family and friends,
my strength and intellect,
the created world
and galaxies and universes
in which I have my being.

I know I have all this on trust,
and I am accountable to you.

For these good and wonderful gifts
I thank you.
But for every minute of my
living you are giving me
more and more, all good.
Please help me not to spoil your gifts,
but to recognise them
and give true thanks in a life of worship.

Thanksgiving

Let us now praise God, for he is our LORD
and our Maker.
We praise him,
for he only is God.

Let us praise God for giving us the record of his work
among people.
We praise him,
for he only is God.

Let us praise God for caring so much for our lives
that he lived on earth before we were even born, to save us.
We praise him,
for he only is God.

Let us praise God for his complexity and yet
for the simple goodness of his Creation.
We praise him,
for he only is God.

Let us praise God for making humankind so that
we are able to know God who is Almighty.
We praise him,
for he only is God.

Let us praise God for setting us in families,
so that from our earliest years we know the love that is the will of
our Father.
We praise him,
for he only is God.

Let us praise God, that our human words are acceptable in prayer.
We praise him,
for he only is God.

Praise

I don't believe anyone
who says I am a miserable sinner.
Murder, blasphemy, false witness, revenge, sacrifice to idols -
these are not part of my life, God.

But you tell me
that I commit the sin of dishonesty.
I make sacrifices
in order to worship my own dignity and reputation and comfort.
I make false witness
when I pass on interesting and cruel gossip about others.
I enjoy nursing in my heart and mind
thoughts of hate and lust and envy.

These little bricks and pebbles
will build up a great high wall -
so that I cannot reach you and see you and hear you -
just as strong as a few great rocks.

Open my understanding
and help me to see myself
in my greed and conceit and selfishness.
Make me turn away from these "little" sins
and break down with your strength the wall I have made
so that I may enjoy your company
because you, loving God, have made me right.

Penitence

Almighty, Creator God,
forgive me.

I so often forget that the things I enjoy most
are your gifts.
I take them for granted.
I say I am lucky.
I praise myself
for being so clever or so good or so something
so that I have won these things:
the enjoyment of playing and working, of labour and leisure,
satisfaction from good food
pleasure of looking at people and places,
friendship and love.

You have given to all people appetites and desires;
for food, for beauty,
for appreciation and thanks from others,
for sex and for song,
for clothing and shelter and safety and daring.
And you have given right and good ways
of satisfying all these desires.

Help me, my Saviour,
to remember that you are with me for good
in everything I plan and do.
Then my life will be praise and worship.

Confession

Each yesterday of life
provides a foundation and a plan for what is built today,
so help me, O God,
to build truly.

By forgiving my sins,
clear the way for what I do today,
so that the coming hours
will prepare for a better tomorrow.

Help me to hear
what you are saying about my past;
help me to hear
the advice you will give me today;
help me to see the future
as also being part of your kingdom already loved by you
so that I may be a partner
in your eternal purpose.

The whole of life is yours, God,
not only what we see;
all glory was yours,
all glory is yours now,
all glory ever shall be yours
for you only are eternal.

Confession

If I put a battery in my torch, God of power,
and then find it doesn't work,
and I look in and see a piece of paper over the terminal,
I think I am a fool.
How can there be light if the path for power is blocked?

And then I look at my life and all around me.
When you said: "Let there be light"
there was light, and you saw that it was good.
And you look at me and say "Let there be light"
because you want your light to shine in me
so that I can see and I can give light to others.

Why is the light so dim, LORD?
Why aren't things brighter for my presence?
Why isn't there more joy and peace and hope when I am present?

I have put a block in the way.
My sin prevents your power flowing through;
your Holy Spirit is the source of power
and my life could be illuminated for me and for others
but sin is the block.

Only a little bit; only a tiny sin; I can manage not to see it at all.
Taking without asking; receiving without thanking;
using someone else without thought for them;
sitting still or interfering; speaking or keeping silence;
I knew it should have been otherwise.

Please forgive me, LORD;
scrape away the insulation and open the path for your power;
let there be light in me for myself and others,
and see that it is good.

Penitence

LORD of the nations,
Lord of earth and heaven,
we do praise you O God.

We do praise you, O Father.
You are our Lord,
the Lord of history, the Judge of all ages.

We do praise you, O Holy Spirit.
You are our Lord,
the Lord of all truth, the Lord of all worship.

We do praise you, O God.
You are the LORD,
the Lord of Creation
from before the beginning to beyond the end.

Help us to put away
our pride, our prejudices and our pettiness.
Help us not only to say "LORD, LORD"
but to live in perfect obedience to you.
Help us to start again
this day
to try to live this prayer.

To you be all praise and service,
for you are King.

Praise and Penitence

Partial Conversations

Genesis 1: 1 - 2: 3

You saw that it was all very good, LORD.

And the people who told your story so long ago
have it all in order
and every stage is good
and you are satisfied.

When you look at our disorder,
at what we have done with the power you entrusted
to us,
do you still see that it is all very good?
Does our stewardship satisfy you?

We acknowledge that we are eager to see error,
we are happy to complain
and we wallow in the negative,
but in truth - in your Truth - we have abused our powers
and misused our home.

In your story,
when you had seen all that you had made you rested.
When you see what we have made
do you need even more recovery?

No. We can pain you by our disobedience
but we cannot weary you
and your creation is still good.
Help us to rejoice and celebrate,
to honour you and live to your glory;
then you will see that all is very good
and we shall know your peace.

Order & Disorder

Genesis 12: 1-9

Abraham must have found it very difficult to do just what you told him to do, and to believe all your promises. But he did obey and he did believe.

We thank you for the faith of Abraham, LORD, for his partnership in all that you planned and did through his life. We thank you because Abraham's faith with little knowledge has made it possible for us to have greater knowledge of you, of your teaching and your work.

Please make our faith strong, LORD God.
When you want us to get out of our comfortable habits,
help us to have the faith to obey and to make our own pilgrimage into adventure.

Make our lives a source of blessing for all who come after us, so that they will find a better land and will worship you as their Leader, Guide and God.

Help us still to journey in faith and to seek first your Reign.

Faith & Obedience

I Kings 18: 7-19

You must have given Elijah a very strong sense of your power and loving presence, LORD, for him to go and stand in danger as he did. When he knew the message you gave him, he must also have known the courage you gave him to meet your enemies and his, and to speak clearly. He was not just a fool; he was a loyal servant.

We do not have the same dangers, but still we are afraid of unkindness and rude and cruel words, and we do not want to stand alone in the right.
Forgive this fear, LORD, and make us strong. When we are willing to deliver your message, then we will hear you.

Help us to be both brave and true, so that we may speak clearly in teaching people what we understand of you; and so that we too may speak with courage but also with gentleness, to encourage and not to despise or belittle.

Give life and humble power to your Church, LORD, and include us in our own requests, so that we may speak your word and be faithful.

Loyalty & Courage

Psalm 23

My whole life long
can be with you, Jesus,
because your promises are upheld by your power.
It is your own word
that you are the Good Shepherd;
that one who lays down his life for the sheep,
the one who keeps the ninety-nine safe and searches for the stray,
the one who knows each by name and calls every one.

I shall want nothing that is necessary
if I follow you.
I shall have wisdom to see what is needful
if I follow your teaching.
So, Lord, help me to hear your call,
to see the way you lead me,
to accept your gifts,
and to be one of your flock for joy throughout my life.

Psalm 46

They don't put you in the headlines, God.
The radio, television, newspapers and magazines
all bring us news
of the tumult and devastation and quaking of the earth
and of our nations and societies.

If this is all we take in, O God,
we shall be brainwashed and think that nothing is safe,
nothing sure and reliable.

But the reporters and photographers and editors
leave you out of the news
about your own world.
Good news doesn't sell the product;
hope is not marketable.
Don't let us leave you out of our thoughts
and perceptions.
Help us to know that you are with us,
our high stronghold,
and that if we stand firm in your gospel
we shall stand firm in your world
and as your servants
see your righteousness maintained through all troubles.

Holding to Truth

Psalm 67

This ancient prayer is our prayer too, LORD.

Be gracious to us and bless us,
but let us not ask
that your blessing stops at us;
through us may your gospel and your salvation
become known to all who know us.

As you are generous, help us to be generous;
not hoarding your gifts for a few as though you love
only those we like.
Help us to share what we have from you
with all people:
those who are strangers,
those who are different,
those who seem unlikeable.

Then, as we make known to the people we meet
your love and blessing,
your praise will sound round your world.

Be gracious to all;
bless all, for we know you love all.

Generous Love

Psalm 107

It is good to give thanks
to you, O LORD;
our thanks join with the gratitude of all people of the world
of all times of the world.
Your power is almighty and eternal and infinite
for you are God.

Those who were lost and homeless,
those who were in the darkness of prison,
those who were fools, choosing evil,
all turned to you and you helped them.
And still you are near to all who need you.

When we feel lost in a changing society,
when we are in the darkness of despair,
when we are fools,
remind us to trust you and ask for your help.

Do not let us forget the help we have had from you -
our salvation in Christ,
our strengthening in daily doubts,
our guidance at times of choosing -
but help us again to join in the thanks
of people in all places and all times
for your enduring love,
so that we are part of the never-ending stream of those
who honour you.

Being Known

Psalm 119: 105

So, God, you are not offering
a bed-side night light
nor a security beam to warn off intruders
so that I can feel good where I am.
You are expecting me
to be on the move,
treading ways I do not know,
risking the unfamiliar,
uncertain of where I am going
and not too confident about the way I am to take.

A useful light does not shine on me
nor be bright upon my eventual goal
but it lights up just that pace ahead of me;
if I step bit by bit towards the light you give
I will get there - safely if uncertainly -
in the end.

You've done it again, God.
Your promise of guidance and effective company
is sure,
but I've got to be mobile and moveable and moving
to stay with your light
to live by your Word;
it is not enough to be stagnant,
to stay in dim withdrawal.

Help me to get up
and set my spiritual feet and my physical feet
on the path you are showing me.

Guidance

Proverbs 3: 13-23

LORD, we so often want to be clever,
and we like to boast of our knowledge of facts,
but you don't seem to think too highly of these things.
Wisdom is your greater gift,
it is your tool of creation
and it is the source of our happiness, the way to good life.

Help us, please, Holy Spirit,
to seek and to find this wisdom;
to recognise good and evil,
to understand your ways with your world,
to learn from you, the God of wisdom and truth.

Then we will have a right judgment;
with your help we will find a way through difficulties and doubts
and we will see clearly in our lives
the riches of peace and honour and deep security.

For your word of wisdom,
loving Creator God,
we thank you.

Wisdom

Isaiah 31: 1-3

They didn't think you could cope
with the situation in Isaiah's time, LORD,
and today's people are just as foolish.

Forgive us for thinking that when trouble comes
it is our wisdom and our activities that will save us.
We are people of this age and think we are clever
and able to control our world and ourselves.

We do not send for horses and chariots
but we strive for certificates and expertise;
we pursue our politics and we stress our strength and we are sure
there is a fix if only we knew where to look;
and we treat you as though you do not know your way
round your own world as it is now.
We seem to think that a God of yesterday
is not the God of today and tomorrow.

Forgive our stupid arrogance, LORD.

Teach us to value knowledge and possessions
and society and strength
only so far as they serve your will,
and help us to look for you and to accept your guidance
in all parts of our living.
Eternal God, this is your time and your world;
show us how to work with you.

Folly & Arrogance

Isaiah 61: 1-4

O God, this prophet of long ago was so clear in knowing what you wanted him to do. Because he had the power of your Spirit he had an understanding of the need to serve and to encourage his neighbour.

Our Saviour Jesus also knew that this same work was his too, and all his life was active love, when his deeds were even greater than his words, signs stating your love.

And now, God, we have your promise that your Holy Spirit will strengthen each one who turns to you as Jesus calls us to follow him as disciples.

Please, God, give us faith and courage to spread good news, to proclaim both liberty and your reign, and to raise the spirits of your people so that they can hope again and see that your will is for our renewal.

We cannot be really joyful on our own, God; give us your strength according to our need in the life to which you call us.

Loving Service

Jeremiah 1: 1, 4-10

LORD, leadership is something
for which you choose your people.
It is not in any way something for which we can praise ourselves:
no source of pride or boasting or pompous bossiness.

If we understood as well as Jeremiah
just what your service means,
we too might try to make our excuses and edge away quietly.
But that wouldn't work either;
when you call us and catch us we stay caught.
Escape from you is running into miserable slavery.
And so, calling God, we thank you for your calling.

We thank you for the work we are strengthened to do
among your people;
for the understanding you give of problems and hopes;
for giving us the patience we need for dealing with people,
for dealing with church authorities,
for dealing with our own weaknesses,
and for coping with the structures.

Help us, Lord Jesus,
to see what is worth spending time and energy on.
Make each one a careful listener
so that we do not waste time ignoring what others say.
Help us to keep quiet if we add nothing but noise.
Help us to contribute without fear or shyness when we can carry
your work forward.

Give to those who lead us the patience to listen and wisdom to
shut us up when that is needed.
Make this time together a road for your Holy Spirit
so that when we finish we may be friends with each other and
with you, so that we may live and work to your glory.

chosen to serve

Jeremiah 31: 31-34

Righteous and merciful God, we must trust you because if we cannot do that there is nothing left to give meaning and sanity to life.

You promised to make a covenant with each one of us, a special relationship in which you are my God and I belong to you because I know you. Jesus made this new covenant strong, and I do know you in my heart: I must love you and my neighbour.

Forgive me for the times I have not trusted you:
forgive me for the times when I have not acknowledged that you are my God:
make your message clearer within me,
make your Spirit strong for my weakness,
and give me the joy of knowing you.

And then, covenant God, I can find what you want me to do with my life and I shall be able to obey.

This we ask because of the promise of Jesus in the new covenant that you will hear each one of us if we ask in his name.

Within the Covenant

Ezekiel 37: 1-14

When Ezekiel and his people had given up hope,
Living LORD, you gave them a guarantee of your presence and a promise of life and hope.

They thought they were forgotten, prisoners of a foreign people, punished and left without any chance of being brought into freedom. Then you gave Ezekiel your word, and you did as you promised.

The thoroughly, totally, finally dead were renewed.

Help us not to be sorry for ourselves, Living LORD, forgetting that your power to save is still as great now as it was then. Our troubles are not so serious, we have lain down in apathy rather than been defeated in conflict. We ought to trust you more than Ezekiel could, because we have heard the Good News of Jesus Christ and know that he was raised from death for our sakes.

Take the dry abandoned bones of the people, of the nation and the Church, and breathe into us your Spirit of Life. Stir again those who have forgotten the pulse of challenge and righteous change, so that we may discover joy in living, and in living may serve you.

LORD God, you know that these bones can live: raise us from despair and surrender so that we may know that you are God of the living.

New Life

Micah 4: 1-4

O God, you are God of all peoples.

You created all humankind,
you have given your word to all peoples and you offer your salvation to each person.

When you have chosen one special people
it has been for serving and for suffering,
not for pride and ease.

Your will has been to bring everyone to you,
to worship you, to serve you,
to be just and righteous for you,
to offer peace to each other for you.

Make us safe from fear, our God,
and help us to live in your peace.
Help us to think first about you,
to seek first to serve you,
and to give you our loyalty,
so that we may find ourselves with all peoples
turning together to you in worship and service
and in this worship we will find the unity and peace
that you will for all humankind.

Human Unity

Matthew 5: 3-10

Happiness, blessedness, joy:
this is the gift you want us to accept,
good Lord Jesus,
the way of life you
showed in your own living
and desired for others.

Clear from our thoughts
the feeling that if we follow you we are moving
from lightness to heaviness,
from being happy sometimes to being solemn and joyless.

Help us to accept and believe your word
that the Kingdom of God is a life of rejoicing,
and that obedience to your will
brings a depth and a strength of joy
that cannot be diminished by the pressures of the world.

Bring us to this blessedness which you promise
by leading us to seek a life suited to your words,
so that believing is in living.

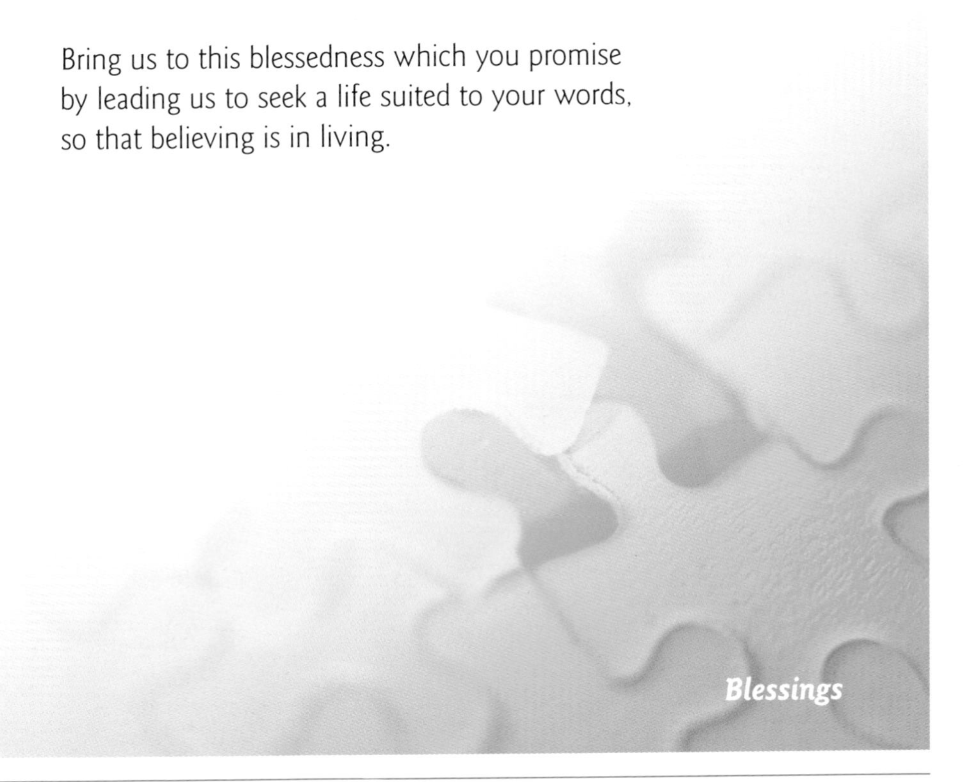

Luke 2: 8-20
(Advent)

One driving ambition
is to be "an elder" - one with authority,
respected, even feared by others
who will be inferior to us.

But you, Almighty God, became a little baby
in the middle of a dangerous world.
If your mother had neglected you,
or if bacteria or accident had struck,
you were helpless - you could have died.

Through this low position and this humble beginning
your power makes us pure.
Please, good Lord Jesus,
help us to examine our ambitions again.

Teach us that kind of humility, that sort of modesty and submission to others
which clears our way to share your work.
Then we can call on your infinite power
and serve in your victorious government,
your servants and the servants of our neighbours
to increase the joy in the world.

Humble Authority

John 6: 41-51

Your life was full of giving, Lord,
giving without payment
and giving without keeping anything back.
Even your life was given,
once in the stable and again on the cross,
so that we might receive hope and strength and salvation.

Keep us from the sin of those enemies
who tried to reduce you to something
they could fully analyse and describe and control and despise.
Let us not talk in shallow modern terms
of proof and observation and scientific laws -
as though that is the fullness of knowledge -
when all we are doing is hiding
from the knowledge that you are God,
Creator and LORD of all,
each one of us.

Help us to that depth of belief
where we can put our own lives into the experiment of obedience
so that in you, Lord Jesus, we can meet and know God,
and in the living bread that you offer
we may find the quality of life that has no limit.

Total Giving

John 15: 1-8

Are we really as close to you
as that, Lord?

Gaining our life from you;
bearing your fruit for you;
making your growth for you.

We know we depend on you.
Without you we are feeble and dry;
unless you enliven us we are dead;
you hold us together to give us unity and shape -
we know that we need you.

But are we really so vital a part
of your being and your work?
Is it our fruit
that becomes the centre of your communion
and the means of our thanksgiving for your renewed life?

If you call us to be servants,
that still leaves us safely separated.
When you invite us to be your co-workers
we are drawn within your purpose
but we are still apart.
But you make us,
for our life time,
a living part of your purpose
organically one with you.

So, green us with your life
that we might live
and bear sweet fruit.

Being One with Christ

John 21

Does this mean, Lord,
that we may find you in the fish and chip shop?
Even if it's run by Muslims or Buddhists
or people of no religion at all?
Are you interested in ordinary activities like eating and drinking;
shopping and cooking and washing up;
earning and spending money?

You chose to meet your disciples by a cooking fire,
after helping them to catch fish to eat and sell.
You cooked for them and shared the meal.
You had been dead, and God's power of creation raised
you, and you cooked for your friends.

We're not surprised
they were too scared to admit that they knew you.
We often try to convince ourselves that you are not our Lord,
standing by us, watching us, offering, eager to help us.

This frightened lot of disciples by the lakeside
discovered that you had found them.
Then they knew that you were looking after them.
Then they knew that you had work for them to do,
in the ordinary busy-ness of life.

In their day's work you were there;
in their rest and play and leisure you were there;
in their friendships and casual contacts, there you were.

Open our eyes and our minds as you opened theirs,
and help us to see that you are with us
every day and every moment of our lives -
and you will guide us and go with us in your service.

real living

Acts 10: 34-35

You have no favourites, LORD,
but you do show partiality -
you love people, each and every one.

We recreate with a ranking and a preference.
We are partial to people like ourselves;
people who will affirm that we are top,
we are the right kind,
we deserve better treatment and a bigger share.

What a blow it was to Peter.
If the unclean were acceptable to you
the unthinkable must be right for him.
He must have felt sick in his stomach
until he realised that his heart was joyful
and he saw yet again how broad and deep is your love,
how rich your realm is.

You had something to say about planks in the eye, Lord.
Something about removing our chunks of wilful blindness
before we pick nits about other people.
And there was a teaching about loving our neighbour.

Help us to love
so that we can accept whoever you accept;
accept and welcome and get to know and to appreciate.
When we know we are chosen,
remind us that we are chosen for service
for all.

All-embracing Love

Acts 17

O LORD, help us to know you.
We cannot know you so as to control you:
    teach us not to want this.
We cannot know you so as to be equal to you:
    teach us not to want this.
We cannot know so as to be able to answer all questions:
    teach us not to want this.

But it is not your will to be an unknown God.
Help us to know you
in whatever way you will reveal yourself.
Help us to know you
in your work of creation of all worlds and of this world
of beauty and order and excitement.
Help us to know you
in all humankind of different languages and customs and understandings,
all offered in the one service of love.
All Creation is yours, but you are more than all Creation.

Help us to know you in our own being:
to know your guidance for our desires;
to see your will for our salvation;
to feel your Holy Spirit working in us;
to be at one with you so that we may know you
with intellect and emotion and body.

You are within us but we cannot contain you;
we are within you but you are not us.
Be known to us, God; our origin and our being and our end,
so that others may know you through your light in us
and through our love for you and for all people
in each person we meet.

knowing God

Romans 5: 1-11

LORD, we are afraid of dying because we cannot see where we are going. We are afraid of suffering because we can see what that is in our own experience.

Yet, Jesus, you suffered and died for us. You didn't even know us, and we do not even obey you, but when you could have escaped you chose to accept capture and give your life so that we can be set free even though we are guilty.

Lord, keep this understanding in our spirits and in our minds; that we have been put right by your suffering and death in your innocence.

Then give us enough faith so that whenever we have to face difficulty or suffering for your sake, your Holy Spirit will guide us through. And even death will not be so terrible because you have been there first.

Because Christ died for us, we can find hope and rejoicing in every part of our own lives.

To you be glory and praise, LORD God our Saviour.

Living in Hope

Romans 8: 18-25

Almighty God, all of creation is waiting for you, eager for you to make everything perfect again.

We are so used to thinking of ourselves as your best work that we forget we are only part of the picture you made, and indeed we are often the part that spoils the whole. Forgive us, LORD, for our forgetfulness and our selfish greed.

We spoil the earth and the plants,
we rip up the earth to obtain minerals and just leave the waste,
we ignore the needs and well-being of wild and domestic animals,
we pollute the soil and the waters and the sky with our rubbish;
and all this is our own doing from our own greed in our own home.
And creation groans, hoping for salvation and freedom,
just as we do.

Forgive us, LORD;
open our eyes to see what we are doing
and give us faith to obey your will,
so that we may reconciled with each other,
with all your work,
and with you.

Creation is God's

Romans 12: 1-8

Thank you, LORD, for making us different.
Life would be terrible if we were all the same;
there would be no variety in what we see,
no chance to help others through our own skills,
no chance to learn, no chance to develop,
no enjoyment of what people offer,
no chance of change.

Help us to see that this variety
is not only your generous gift for our enjoyment;
it is also your plan for the way in which we may serve you..
Help us each to see plainly the gift we have,
and to offer this gift in our life to you.
so that for each of us this may be our true worship.
Then help us to see, to value
and to accept
the different gifts of our neighbour.

You have been generous to me, LORD,
help me to be generous with myself,
loving you and loving my neighbour,
and finding this love expressed in serving and accepting.

In the name of Jesus,
we ask you to bless us.

Generous Variety

Revelation 3: 14-21

It is easy to listen to this strong criticism and judgment of others, Lord Jesus, and to see how true it is, how well deserved. Lukewarm tastelessness is not what you call for!

These are people who want to keep all their privileges, who refuse to share their power and wealth with us, but who like to use your name on Sundays. They are not really ready to give whatever it costs, neither are they openly against you. They want it both ways!

We don't like them, Lord, because we want what they have and so we cheer when you say you reject them.

Forgive us, Lord.
We are not really bothered about their relationships with you,
only about their behaviour towards us.

Forgive us, Lord.
We hang on to our privileges and we fight hard to gain more,
and we will not share,
and we like to use your name as our comfort,
and we like to keep our eyes closed,
and we love our profitable sins.

Give us grace, Lord,
helping us to take risks
to find peace and joy in fellowship with you.

Good is for All

Offering & Commitment

O LORD, help me to pray:
to know that you are interested and listening,
to know that you are eager to help,
to know that you gave me the wish to pray.

Help me to offer you
all my thoughts and desires,
even those which do not seem to be prayers.
Take them, God,
because they are a real part of me,
and use them to lead me to you.

Help me, in my turn, to listen,
so that in whatever experiences I hear you
I may recognise and know and respond.

For help in prayer

When the first rains fall after drought,
and the ground is cleaned and freshened,
we rejoice in the scent and the sight.
Holy Spirit, make my life clean and fresh
so that I may be a cause of rejoicing
for you and for my neighbour.

Wash away the dry dust of my selfishness.
Bring to life the seeds of love
that you have kept within me all the time.
Make me fertile with ideas and means of serving others
and of truly worshipping you.

I cannot put myself right
any more than
a desert can make itself green with life;
and so, living Spirit,
I must ask you
to do all that is necessary
to bring forth my response,
to make my life good to see
and to share and to live.
Break the drought
which is a life without the power of your love,
and refresh my spirit.

Life refreshed

Peter was a rock
but that was a rock that you placed, Jesus;
that was a rock that you promised to build on.

A rock in the wrong place is a nuisance;
people trip, hurt themselves, turn from the path.
But you were once called the Stone that the builders rejected,
now the strength of the new building
chosen and carefully placed.

Help us in our work when we meet those
who think of themselves as stony-hearted, unmoveable,
resistant to all effects of development and change.
Help us first to see the usefulness of each one
in the building of your kingdom.
Then fill us with love:
strong enough to persevere against the hardest face;
gentle enough to flow over and around the roughness;
persevering, teaching, healing.
So that we may bring your peace to a troubled life
and make plain in our life, in our relationships,
that your love has room for all
so that no one is a lonely island remote from your kingdom.

Use us as foundations, Lord Jesus,
to be seen or unseen according to your will,
so that on our work may be built your fellowship
in which each person will find a place to belong in your name.

Help us today to work together, to learn together,
to play together,
so that your Holy Spirit can be at work among us all
and through each one of us.

Stable Strength

Almighty and merciful God,
help us to find our place in your Kingdom.

We cannot expect to be citizens of that Kingdom
through any quality of our own.
Our wisdom is not enough.
Our obedience is not enough.
Our goodness is not enough.
We are not Christs;
we cannot satisfy any tests for citizenship.

But we can rejoice,
knowing that it is your love,
not our (non-existent) perfection,
which brings us into your Kingdom
seeking asylum and refuge by grace and not by right.

Help us, then, to find strength and hope;
help us to know how infinite is your power
and to see that this same authority and power is focused
by your love on each one of us.

Receive us;
enable us to offer you all praise and service,
for you are our King.

Citizenship in God's Realm

Creator God, we offer to you
the materials of our living.

You have given us all that we are
and all that we have
for the work and play of life.
From your creation we take the wood and the metal,
the paper and ink, the cloth and all we use.
It is through your generosity
that we have life and understanding and skills.

Help us to show our gratitude
through what we do and who we are
so that our acts may follow our words.

May your Kingdom come
and may we obey your will for us.
May your Kingdom come
and may we be part of its coming.
May your Kingdom come
and may our lives show us to be people of the Kingdom.

To you be all praise and service
for you are King and Judge of your creation.

Self Offering

We need to serve you, God,
so that we may enjoy the privilege
of working with you.
Help us to look for you and your Kingdom today,
in this place, with these people;
the people around us,
the people we are to serve
in your service.

Take me into your service, O King,
make me one of your subjects.
Take me with my doubts;
help me to offer them for you to use.
Take me with my fears;
show me that your strength is necessary and sufficient.
Take me with my sins;
accept even them to make me clean and fit.

Show me the way of service.
Speak to me through friend and book
and my own experience and thought.
Teach me the customs of your people and of your Kingdom
that I may be welcome.

To you be all praise and honour and service,
for you are King.

Willing Service

LORD, God, it is not a light matter
to declare myself to be one of your people.

Life has many temptations and attractions
and I can make myself so busy that I forget you,
the Ruler and Giver of life.

Help me,
to pray humbly, to learn truly, to live sincerely,
and in all living
to love you and all your children.

I want to receive your gifts,
and I want to give myself to you.

Hear my prayer, LORD God,
and help me to recognise your answer.

Self Offering

Lord, I believe; help my unbelief.
Accept me as one of your followers,
accept my uncertainties
and my doubts and my questions,
my failures and my unworthiness,
my ambition
and my potential to be what you desire.

When I forget to pray, forgive me.
When I trust myself instead of you, forgive me.
When I am self-centred, make me look outwards.

Because you made me,
and gave life to my body and spirit,
because you love me
and have made promises to me,
save me from the sin which will be my unaided choice,
and make me yours.

Moving Towards God

LORD God, a student is always in danger
of thinking that study and application and success
is the sufficient way to become good and admirable.
How easy it is to think that all that is needful for life
is available through careful application
to books and data banks.

Forgive this pride and arrogance, LORD.
Help us to learn from the people of old
that education is in the whole of our living,
not just in what we can cram into our intellects.

Educate us Lord Jesus;
bring us to fulfilment as the people you would have us be.
You are the Way, the Truth and the Life,
the Light of the world,
and if we are to be of any use to ourselves and to others
we need to learn to live by the light of your truth.

Make us fit to be with people,
make us humble to learn with others,
humble with our own knowledge,
humble with the power we gather.
Make us pure to be used in your plan for living,
and make our lives full and helpful in your world.
Teach us to desire excellence and to love service
for the sake of Jesus, called Teacher.

Growing in Service

Jesus Christ,
St Paul tells us that you once said
that it is more blessed to give than to receive.
It is good to stop and think about your gifts to us:
the blessings of food and water,
shelter and care and comfort,
knowledge and understanding and expectation,
friends and fellowship and strangers.

Make us gracious and grateful receivers,
knowing our dependence on you and on other people,
and therefore willing to give from our riches.

Help us too, to receive what you want to give us:
challenge and guidance, renewal and perseverance,
neighbours to love and strangers to nourish,
faith strong for obedient action,
the call to discipleship in the strength that you promise.

And teach us how to give,
not looking for profit and repayment and pleasure and fame;
if we are selfish and concerned only with ourselves,
we are of no use in creating community.
Help us to give time and thought and effort and sympathy
as our neighbours need these from us,
even if the giving is costly.
Then, Lord, we shall indeed be blessed in our giving.

Blessed Receiving

Lord Jesus, your disciples called you "Master",
and they were right to do so.
Your hearers and your questioners called you "Good Teacher",
and they also were right.

Jesus, be our Master and Teacher,
so that all we meet and experience in work and play,
in labour and leisure,
may be tested by your truth
and inform us so that we may grow in you.

Help us, so that we do not keep you only to prayer times,
but so that we can see your glory and your mercy,
your strength and your justice and righteousness,
as we learn from the world in which we live,
the world you made and the world which you claim.

Then, Lord,
we will have true knowledge and rich understanding,
and in joy we can praise you worthily
in all our living.

God our Saviour,
we bring our hearts and minds together in prayer
as we brought our voices together in song.
We thank you for the fellowship of worship,
all the diversities of personalities
all the differences of needs
all the wealth of gifts,
all called together by you to be one in your Spirit.

Accept us, separately and together,
in this time set apart for you,
and by your acceptance make us fit for you
now and in the days to come.

Forgive us for turning away from you,
for trusting our own wisdom and strength
rather than your love,
so that we have hurt people instead of helping them.

As you have promised your forgiveness
loving God,
may we trust you perfectly
and go on in worship
knowing that we have been made whole again.

Congregational Commitment

Loving, Creator God,
you have given your creatures a share of your power;
you have blessed us with the ability to create,
to work with ideas and visions and possibility
to make something new.

You have blessed us with understanding and wonder,
with observation and exploration,
with imagination and skill.

You have blessed us with powers
to honour or to demean
to worship or to desecrate
to increase or to spoil the peace of our neighbours.
And you have set us free to use these powers
according to our judgment.

Bless us also with your guidance.

As you have created all that is
to your glory and for the good of your people,
help us to be your partners in continuing creation,
offering you who we are and what we do
and humble and joyful trust
that we can please you
and love our neighbour as ourselves.

Chosen to be Partners

You know, God, the limitations of our words
in thought and speech and listening.

If we say something should be done,
and then we are satisfied with saying so,
we do not stir ourselves any further.
If we condemn something as evil in society or in self,
and that is sufficient for us,
then we suffer no pains in order to correct it.

We know this is not enough, God.
Jesus told us that it is the doers of your Word
who are your people;
when we don't do, we just echo.
Forgive our lazy feebleness, LORD.

And sometimes we find a word or a phrase or a thought for you
and we want you to be summarised and contained
within that finite human word.
We are angry when you are greater than our terms,
we are dissatisfied when the god we create in our own image
is too small and cannot be God.

Break into our little lives, wonderful God,
and conquer us and set us free
to live your living Word.

From Saying to Being

God, you are Father and Mother to everyone;
but she is our mother.

We thank you for the life that you have given her
and for the lives that she has given us.

We know that she has lived all her life in your sight,
but soon we hope that you will be in her sight
as if face to face
as she adores her Saviour and you bless your child.
You have loved her as you love us;
this love is stronger than death
and we know that your perfect gift is life eternal.

So we commit her to you in faith
and hope.
As you are with her,
be with us in our sorrow,
so that it is savoured with joy in memory
and confidence in expectation.

And then go on with us
as our lives continue,
in the knowledge that you love us
and our mother is with you in peace.

On the Death of a Mother

God, I'm a father.

Yes, I know you know;
you are the giver of all life and each life
and this very particular new life.
But I need to tell what I am just starting
to realise.
I am a father!

Of course I am rejoicing -
I certainly think I am.
But I am anxious too.

It is not so much what silly people say
about losing my freedom because
that is just too selfish to think about seriously.

I am anxious because
Jesus called you Daddy and
Jesus told us to call you Father
so my child is going to learn
about your Fatherhood
through the way I am a father.

This gift of life is glorious
but I need you to help me
to come to terms with what this means for me.

Help me honour you
as I learn from you about parenting
and to come closer to you
for all our sakes.

New Fatherhood

An index of first or indicative lines

	Page
Abraham must have found it very difficult	63
Ah, but our difficulties are so great!	45
All praise belongs to you, O God, Creator	52
Almighty and merciful God, help us to find our place	93
Almighty, Creator God, forgive me	57
Almighty Creator God, Ruler of all space and time,	101
Almighty God, all of creation is waiting for you	85
Almighty God, it is difficult to remember your greatness	20
Are we really as close to you as that, Lord?	80
Christ is Risen!	39
Creator God, although the years change	34
Creator God, we offer to you the materials of our living.	94
Dear God, we use words now	42
Dear God, you have called us together	102
Does this mean, Lord, that we may find you in the chip shop	81
Each new day is your gift, loving living God	10
Each yesterday of life provides a foundation	58
Eternal Father God, on this day of our Saviour's appearance	38
For the gift of the night	5
Generous God take our gifts	21
God, I'm a father.	107
God of all power and wisdom	27
God of life and love	13
God of promise and delivery	31
God our Saviour, we bring our hearts and minds together	103
God who seeks need and gives in love	32
God, you are Father and Mother to everyone	106
Happiness, blessedness, joy	77
Help us now to remember, Lord	17
How can we know that you are here	14
I don't believe anyone who says I am a miserable sinner	56
If a drum is to give rhythm and life	47
If Christ is living now	46

If I put a battery in my torch 59
It has been a good day 26
It is easy to listen to this strong criticism 87
It is good to give thanks to you, O LORD 68
Jesus Christ, St Paul tells us 99
Jesus said, "Love God 4
Let us now praise God, for he is our LORD 55
Let us praise God, our Maker and Lord 18
LORD God, a student is always in danger 98
LORD, God, it is not a light matter 96
LORD God of love, we bring you our praise 29
Lord, I believe; help my unbelief. 97
LORD, I do not know what today will bring 3
Lord Jesus, accept what I have done today, 15
Lord Jesus Christ, there is nothing very much 6
Lord Jesus, you taught the people your truth 44
Lord Jesus, your disciples called you "Master", 100
LORD, leadership is something for which you choose 73
LORD of the nations 60
Lord, on the day when we remember your entry into Jerusalem 35
LORD, we are afraid of dying 84
LORD, we so often want to be clever 70
Loving, Creator God,you have given your creatures a share 104
Loving, generous God prodigal with your love 11
Loving, generous God, you give us more than we can measure 53
Loving God, our Creator, Judge and Saviour 12
My understanding is limited, O God 54
My whole life long can be with you, Jesus 65
O God, LORD of day and night, 19
O God of mercy, as the year draws to its close 33
O God, our Father and Friend 22
O God, this prophet of long ago was so clear 72
O God, you are God of all peoples 76
O LORD, help me to pray 90
O LORD, help us to know you. 83
O Lord of the dance, yours is a dance of life 30

One driving ambition is to be "an elder" 78
Peter was a rock 92
Pressures are strongest when they are subtle 50
Righteous and merciful God, we must trust you 74
Ruler of time and space 8
So, God, you are not offering a bed-side night light 69
Thanks be to you, Lord Christ 9
Thank you, God .. for giving me the morning 16
Thank you, LORD, for making us different. 86
Thank you, speaking God 43
The care of a chiropodist 36
The Lord Jesus takes care of us 24
The night has ended 2
They didn't think you could cope 71
They don't put you in the headlines, God 56
This ancient prayer is our prayer too, LORD 67
To you, LORD God, we now commend ourselves 23
Was it just the enthusiasm of the early days, Lord 40
We need to serve you, God 95
We rise in the morning 7
When Ezekiel and his people had given up hope 75
When the first rains fall 91
When we think of the day we have enjoyed 25
When you came with your disciples 48
When you've got your telly and a full belly 49
Where is the midwife, Jesus? vi
Where would I have been, Lord 37
You have filled today with good things for me 28
You have no favourites, LORD 82
You know, God, the limitations of our words 105
You must have given Elijah a very strong sense 64
You saw that it was all very good, LORD 62
Your life was full of giving, Lord 79

103 prayers